This book belongs to:

The Shy Monster

Written by: Shamirrah Hill, M.A.

Illustrated by: Donald L. Hill, MBA
(Donnie Graphics)

Published by Shamirrah Hill
Phoenix, AZ

Library of Congress Control Number: 2017912924

Copyright © 2017 by Shamirrah Hill LLC

All Rights Reserved. No part of this publication may be reproduced or transmitted in any form or by any means, electronic or mechanical, including photocopying and recording, or by any information storage or retrieval system without written permission from the copyright owner.

Printed in the United States of America
ISBN-13: 978-0-692-93805-8

Dedication

This book is dedicated to my mom, Phyllis Tremble-Hardin, who encouraged me to break out of my shyness when I was a child. She pushed me to try new things that got me out of my comfort zone and she always supported my creative endeavors.

Mom, thank you for always being my cheerleader and number one fan. I can now pour out into the world what you poured into me.

SPECIAL THANKS TO:

God, the source of my creativity.

My husband, Donald Hill, for inspiring me and partnering with me to bring this book to life.

The Donnie Graphics team, Youmie Jean-Francois, Rashana Underwood, Dr. Telpriore Tucker, and Tanisia Avent for their feedback and contributions.

All of my friends, family members, and teachers who encouraged and supported me throughout my life journey.

All of the supporters who purchased this book for themselves or for children who will benefit from its empowering message.

Do you know the shy monster? He makes me feel shy.
I can't speak around him, and I don't know why.

When I want to speak up and be very brave,
The shy monster comes and makes me afraid.

Sometimes I want to ask questions in class,
But the shy monster tells me that people will laugh.

He says I'll look silly and feel really bad,
And people will tease me and make me feel sad.

Teacher, I want to understand,
but I'm just too shy to raise my hand.

Cheerleading try-outs are happening, and I really want to go.
I wish I could be a cheerleader and be a part of the show.

I wish I could cheer and flip and kick and jump and dance around.
I wish I could shake my pom-poms and get lifted off the ground.

But the shy monster said, "You won't make it. Don't even bother to try.
You'll mess up all of the moves. You'll fall down and you'll cry!"

Coach, I wish I could be on the team,
but I'm just too shy to go after my dream.

At lunch time, I feel lonely as I watch the others play. I wish I had more friends, but I don't know what to say.

One time, I tried to make a friend, but I got really scared. I tried to speak, but my words got stuck, so I just stood there and stared!

I stared as I heard the shy monster's words: "You're going to say the wrong thing. If you speak, you will embarrass yourself!" The shy monster is so mean!

Some days I feel sad when I eat lunch all alone.
I want to be with others, but I feel safer on my own.

I want to be your friend; it's true,
but I'm just too shy to talk to you.

My mom noticed my shyness and had a talk with me.
She said, "Being shy is like being in jail; I want you to be free...

You have to speak up and go after your dreams and have fun and be yourself. I signed you up for an acting class. I really believe it will help."

My acting teacher and the other students welcomed me to the class. When it was my turn to speak or perform, they promised not to laugh.

My acting teacher, Ms. Hill, asked, "Is the shy monster talking to you?" I said, "Yes! How did you know?" She said, "It used to talk to me too...

I know it seems big and scary right now, but I'm going to help you through this. It's time to defeat that shy monster, and I'm going to help you do this!

The shy monster is a bully and it says things that are not true. You must stop believing the shy monster and start believing in you.

When the shy monster tries to silence you or stop you from chasing your dreams, you face that mean old shy monster and you tell him all of these things:

Shy monster, your voice can't hurt me. I do not believe what you say. You can say scary things if you want to, but I'm going to speak up anyway. My voice will keep getting bigger and your voice will keep getting small. I am brave enough to express myself. I am not shy at all."

I told the shy monster these things, and he started to get very small. The more I spoke up, the smaller he got, and I started to feel strong and tall.

After I finished my acting class, I felt very happy and free. I finally believed in myself and I finally could be me!

Now, when the shy monster tries to scare me, I do not let him win. I know that my ideas are great and I know I am stronger than him.

I express my ideas and I chase my dreams and I am not afraid to fall. Cause I know if I fall, I can get back up, and it's not a big deal after all.

I say "Hi," to my classmates now, and they say "Hi," back to me. I ask if they want to play with me and they say "Yes," happily.

Just like that, we become friends and we have lots of fun. Now we eat lunch together and we play outside in the sun.

In class, when I have questions now, I raise my hand and ask. It helps me understand things so I can complete my tasks. One day, my classmate said to me, "Your question helped me understand. I had that same question, but I was too shy to raise my hand."

I smiled at him and said, "I used to be shy too. If I can beat the shy monster, you can beat him too."

My grades are better, I have more friends, and oh, there's one more thing! After I performed with my acting class, I made the cheerleading team!

Shy monster, your voice can't hurt me. I do not believe what you say. You can try to scare me, but I'm chasing my dreams anyway. My voice will keep getting bigger and your voice will keep getting small. I am brave enough to be myself. I am not shy at all!

Post-Reading Discussion Questions

The following questions are written using language that caters to children in 2nd and 3rd grade. However, these questions may be used for children ranging from 6-10 years old. Parents and teachers are encouraged to use these questions to facilitate discussions that will help children process the story, think about their own challenges with shyness, and increase their self-confidence.

1) What does it mean to chase your dream?

2) In the story we just read, the little girl had more than one dream. One of her dreams was to have more friends. What were some of her other dreams?

3) In the beginning of the story, the little girl did not go after her dreams. Why didn't she go after her dreams?

4) When people are shy, it can feel like there is a voice inside them, telling them that something bad will happen if they speak. It's like hearing the voice of the shy monster. Have you ever felt like the shy monster was talking to you? What did the shy monster say to you?

Teacher/Parent Answers & Talking Points:

Use the talking points below to make sure students are getting the right answers and to help you contribute to the discussion in a way that encourages and supports them

Question #1: Chasing your dreams means going after what you want. You can have a big dream like becoming a famous singer. Or you can have a smaller dream like making a new friend or earning a good grade in class.

Question #2: Her other dreams were to become a cheerleader and to be able to ask questions in class.

Question #3: She didn't go after her dreams because she was shy/scared.

Question #4: The shy monster says mean things just to try to scare you out of going after your dreams. When the shy monster says mean things to you, it's important for you to be brave and go after your dreams anyway. Did you know you can use the same words we heard in the story to help you defeat the shy monster when the shy monster talks to you? Let's try it. It's the shy monster affirmation. Stand up, put your hand on your heart, and repeat after me...

Shy Monster Affirmation

Parents and teachers are encouraged to read this affirmation, one line at a time, and pause after each line so that the child or group of students can repeat each line:

Shy monster, your voice can't hurt me

I do not believe what you say

You can try to scare me

But I'm chasing my dreams anyway

My voice will keep getting bigger

And your voice will keep getting small

I am brave enough to be myself

I am not shy at all

SOCIAL-EMOTIONAL DEVELOPMENT

<u>Tips for Parents of Shy Children</u>

Encourage your child to participate in extracurricular activities.

Encourage your child to participate in a performing arts program that helps kids increase their confidence through the arts.

Encourage play dates (at a friend's house or at your house).

Practice different scenarios at home (meeting a new kid, asking a question in class, etc.).

Encourage your child to rehearse show and tell or other class presentations in front of you at home before presenting at school.

Talk to your child's teacher about your child's shyness. The teacher will likely have some insight based on experiences and observations of your child at school. The two of you can share insights, brainstorm, and create a plan together.

Encourage your child to talk about their fears and try to empathize (i.e. "I feel shy too sometimes.")

Compliment your child often. Tell them things you like about them.

Celebrate your child's victories. When you notice them being brave or making even small improvements, tell them you are proud of them and point out the specific things they did well.

About the Author

Shamirrah Hill, M.A. is a creativity specialist and performing arts program developer with over 15 years of experience. She has a Bachelor's degree in Theatre from Howard University and a Master's degree in Educational Theatre from New York University. As a certified K-12 theatre teacher, she loves teaching acting classes that help children and teens get out of their comfort zones, overcome their shyness, and feel confident. She wrote *The Shy Monster* to empower children to overcome their fears, defeat their shyness, and become who they are meant to be in the world.

Shamirrah is the founder of the Black Youth Theatre Program - an arts program that helps Black youth in Phoenix, AZ, learn about their culture, develop their creativity, and feel comfortable & confident in their skin. She is also a creative writing coach who works with adults and children to help them develop their children's books. She founded the Youth Writer's Academy to help children, ages 9 and up, become published authors.

Shamirrah has performed throughout the country as an actress, dancer, mime, and spoken word artist. She has trained several actors, dancers, mimes, steppers, and poets of various ages. Additionally, she is a director and playwright with work that has been produced and performed in Washington, DC, and New York City.

To learn more about Shamirrah Hill, her Arizona-based programs, or her online courses, visit www.ShamirrahHill.com.

SHAMIRRAHHILL
www.ShamirrahHill.com

www.ingramcontent.com/pod-product-compliance
Lightning Source LLC
Chambersburg PA
CBHW061817290426
44110CB00026B/2896